'Chicken Lyrics~

Jay Sharpe

Copyright © 2015
Bethune Publishing – The Bethune Group
Jay Sharpe Author
First Printing

All rights reserved, including the right to reproduce this work in any form whatsoever without written permission from the publisher, except for brief passages in connection with a review. Photographs may not be reproduced without permission of the owner.

For information write:

Bethune Publishing, Inc.
P. O. Box 2008
Daytona Beach, FL 32115-2008
docbethune@tbginc.org
Jacket designed by
John-Mark McLeod
J2maginations, LLC
J2maginations@gmail.com
Book design and page layout by
Bethune Publishing, Inc.
Printed in the United States of America
Library of Congress Control Number: 2016900986
ISBN 0978-0-9971548-1-8

Just for Jay

"Jay's eloquent and heartfelt quotes are truly inspiring for the Mind, Body & Spirit. This book is filled with compassionate, thought provoking and redemptive insights. I enjoyed every lyric and affirming verse. Anyone looking for a mental boost of daily encouragement should read 'Chicken Lyrics'...a lyrical treasure."

Highland 'Dobby' Dobson OD

Jamaica's legendary Reggae singer of the popular song 'Loving Pauper' & Author of **The Misadventures of Saucy and Her Mama.**

Table of Contents

DEDICATION	3
EPILOGUE	4
FOREWORD	5
MIND	7
BODY	151
SPIRIT	183

~Dedication~

This book is dedicated to the following persons whose support and contribution are unmatched.

My parents- Sylvia & Rupert Sharpe

My children- Chloe' Creed, & Cidney

My Dearest- Jack

My cheerleading team: Maxine-(Seenas), Michael-(Souljah), Maxwell (Bollo), Jacqueline-(Sissy), Mark-(Tootie), Kim, M&M, Safa, Cente', Dianne, Basil, Junior, Colleen, Bert, Dee & Dobby.

My Inspirational team: Janis F. Kearney, The late Alvin Hunter Sr, Eman Jeremiah, Elias Michael and Yanira Destiny.

Special thanks to Cassandra Minott-Berry Esquire for her guidance.

Much appreciation to my publisher Dr. Evelyn Bethune and all my supporters who believe in me and my work and have shown me love.

Thank you!

Be bless

Always,

Jay

Epilogue

To my readers
Thank you for reading 'Chicken Lyrics'. I trust that you will discover a piece of yourself among these pages and I invite you to stay on this journey with me. My hope is that these quotes will inspire you to use your gifts and touch others in a very special way.

You are amazing! You are beautiful! You are gifted! You are perfect, just the way you are! Connect to the inner spirit within and find the best version of yourself and live it each day. I pray that these words will ignite the genius in you, and give you the courage to break out of your shell, gain your wings and soar to new heights.

Be bless~
Always,
Jay~

Foreword

by
Janis F. Kearney
Author, Lecturer, Publisher and Presidential Diarist to U.S. President Bill Clinton

Jay Sharpe's `Chicken Lyrics' is a wonderful and awesome book of poetry, wisdoms, and prophecies. A tightly woven offering of beautiful memories and wise admonitions. There is, within these pages, something for everyone. Poetry and prose. Refreshing, surprising. Thoughts that will surely elicit a smile, and charge our spiritual senses.

Sharpe's seamless transformation from straight English speak to sensuous Island croon is magical. Reminds us of all that we once knew, but long forgot. Brimming with poignant hope, even her verses of dire warnings fail to defeat her uplifting mood.

Whether you read books to learn, to escape reality, or to fall in love with words and sounds inside your mind... `Chicken Lyrics'~ has something for you.

Thankfully, there is much you will surely want to share with others. And, none will you easily forget.

Mind

CHICKEN LYRICS   **JAY SHARPE**

Mind:

Composing words has been a passion of mine for as long as I can remember. It was the only exercise that completely puts me mentally at ease. At age 11, I would curl up in bed, in the bedroom upstairs and shut out the world for as long as it took, to put my thoughts on paper. Often the sound of Mama's voice would come crashing through the door *"Chicken what yuh doin' up deh?"* In addition, I would get strange looks from my siblings…but I quickly became immune to those gestures as my love for writing topped everything. I would write about things I experienced, things that inspired me, things I dreamed of, people I loved and admired…

Writing took me places I could only imagine. I went on a mental journey to faraway places. My imagination soared like an eagle through the clouds of my mind.

I wrote the first quote at 13yrs old, to a boy I loved. ***'This ring is round and has no end, that's how long you and I will be friends.'*** I had read it somewhere and the content suited me fine as It was his birthday. I had saved up all my money to get him a card but I also wanted to put a personal touch to the gift so he would figure out that I liked him a lot. I am blessed to still have him as a friend today.

The mind is a powerful muscle, and when exercise it can be as stronger than an ox. The body depends on the mind to bring forth what the spirit is saying. The mind is not physical it is far more in depth than that. It uses the brain as a vessel to make visible the thoughts. When we tap into our minds and feel the spirit within, then and only then can we be free. ***'Free your mind and the rest will follow'***

CHICKEN LYRICS   **JAY SHARPE**

Choose your altitude by adjusting your attitude.

Garner up a mentality like an eagle. Fly above your adversaries and soar towards all possibilities!

The anti-virus for hate is love. Protect the software of your heart by downloading the power of love in your psyche daily and ensure its upgraded frequently with chips of kindness. This way you will keep out the viruses of naysayers, haters, hackers and the malicious worms and dysfunction. It will also help you to recognize new versions of harmful intent.

A healthy mind cannot reside in an unclean body and a sick soul.

Boredom is a weapon of mass destruction to a young mind.

CHICKEN LYRICS   **JAY SHARPE**

A generalist must not tell a specialist how to do his work.

'Ah cobbler shud never tell ah' architect how fi design di house!' (Jamaican Patois)
#StayInYourLane#JackOfAllTradesMasterOfNone
#KeepingAllEyesOnYou.

'Believe in love & its' endless possibilities'~

'If only we would begin to live 'our truth', what a difference we would make in this world.'

Being vulnerable is one of the most courageous behaviors you can display.

Good things happen to good people, when they do good things for the good of others.

CHICKEN LYRICS **JAY SHARPE**

There's nothing wrong with standing up for your rights!

Not everything that is broken must be thrown away. Sometimes it's worth putting the pieces back together again.

CHICKEN LYRICS   **JAY SHARPE**

It's so important to spend your time wisely, and even more important to spend it with people you love.

If only you believe……..you would be in awe of yourself!

When we center our thoughts on the things that matters the most to us, it really minimizes the size of the adversaries that lurks around us.

Loving is an easy thing to do. It's the people we love, the places we love and the things we love that sometimes makes it difficult.

The things you think of the most today, are the actions that will show up the most in your tomorrow.

CHICKEN LYRICS **JAY SHARPE**

Someday you're gonna.......and then there are some days when you just ain't gonna....

It takes Passion, Persistence & a Plan to reach your goal. Stay on task.

Doors open and close every day; it's just a part of life. It's up to you to recognize when to enter or exit. Be careful! Not every door that opens means 'welcome' and not every one that's closed is 'shutting you out'.

The moment you think you have to "fit in" is the very moment you begin to lose a piece of who you are.

Before your story can inspire others it must be an inspiration to you.

Worrying about being loved is a distraction. Focus on being the lover. Give love and you will receive love.

You don't have to go back to the starting point every time. Start from where you are and just keep moving forward.

Effective communication is vital in every relationship, especially the ones we have with ourselves.

When we appreciate the importance of others in our life, we learn to accept them, flaws and all.

Determination is one of the best qualities to possess.

Why must you settle when you can make another choice?

Love is unconditional! *'Live! Love! Laugh! & Learn!'* :-) *John 4:18 *'There is no fear in love, but perfect love casts out fear. For fear has to do with punishment, and whoever fears has not been perfected in love.'*

Nuff (Many) people are okay with you as long as you are beside them or behind them. The moment you are ahead... all hell breaks loose! #StayFocus&KeepMovingForward

Never apologize for who you are.

Work with what you have, until you can work with what you want or what you want works for you.

CHICKEN LYRICS   **JAY SHARPE**

Parents, the best thing you can do for your children is help them discover their purpose and the only way to do that is to show them how you discovered yours.

Holding on to hurt only hurts you.

The people we attract are a reflection on us; so before you are quick to criticize the people in your life, know that they are around because of you.

Never sacrifice your purpose for anything.

Your skills may get you famous, but your gift will minister to others and should not be used as a platform for fame.

CHICKEN LYRICS   **JAY SHARPE**

If you tell lies to yourself, you will have to live with the lie. Be good to you and be honest.

Life is really strange at times. Sometimes you have to lose something you love in order to find yourself, and then just when you do, you realize that you may also rediscover some of those things you lost.

CHICKEN LYRICS   **JAY SHARPE**

Only a senseless person uses the same weapon to fight his opponent. Yours have to be stronger even if it's only your determination.

Some folks look for the twist in the rope rather than see how carefully the fibers are bonded.

CHICKEN LYRICS   **JAY SHARPE**

Learn to live with standards not limits.

It is only when we learn from our mistakes that we fail forward.

Change the way you speak to yourself (& you know you do) …don't sabotage your ingenuity. When you are happy you are at your best. Happiness is a choice; therefore, choose to say to yourself "I will be happy while …"

CHICKEN LYRICS   **JAY SHARPE**

Listen! There is no better feeling in the world, than the feeling of purpose. To be present in your purpose is cosmic.

When you try to get ahead of others it means you're gonna have to imitate something they have done. Try to get ahead of yourself. Set a goal and stick to it.

Thoughts are actions waiting for your permission to manifest.

Love always wins!

Learn to strengthen your emotional immune system with love and positivity and stay away from people who carry deadly emotional viruses.

'Acknowledge your failures and mis-steps and do all possible to use it as a 'fail forward' lesson. That setback was an opportunity for you to come back.' #WinnersNeverQuit&QuittersNeverWin.

Learn how to stay positive and cope through all circumstances! It is imperative to your growth and your 'move forward', that you do.
#PositiveMindset   #ChangeTheWayYouSeeThings.

CHICKEN LYRICS   **JAY SHARPE**

He who teaches you how to cope has taught you everything.

If I teach you how to cope, I have taught you everything.

"Be original!" When you become a carbon copy of others, you are only delaying The Creator`s construction of your blueprint. #StopDiFallahFashin.

It can be dangerous if certain people discover your full potential before you do. #KnowThyWorth!

Who are you to be killing people because of their preferences? Your hate will never become more powerful than love. Only more love can do that! #EmancipateYourselfFromMentalBigotry #GetWisdom!

Not everyone who is **with** you has earned the right to your intimacy; share only with those who are *for* you.

For it is when we love unconditionally that we truly find ourselves. Love should never let you lose yourself; in fact, it should do the exact opposite.

Close your eyes and dream the impossible, then open your eyes and see the possibilities!

Close your eyes and fall asleep with a dream.................then open your eyes and wake up with a clear plan.

CHICKEN LYRICS   **JAY SHARPE**

Each day we create something that will become a part of our legacy. Make it memorable.

Unless tested you will never know your score.

How else will you know your strength if you are not put to the test?

Don't be afraid to face a conflict or a challenge. Remember if it comes to you, you are equipped to handle it. *#Corinthians 10:13

God has given us the gift to love; we have to make the decision to open it and use it.

Parenting was the best skill I ever learned. Motherhood was the greatest gift I was given.

Children can teach you a lot about life, the unfiltered version.

Your attitude will determine your altitude, and your gratitude will secure it!

Love is the ability to say *"I'm sorry"*....and mean it.
#WithAllHumility&GentlenessWithPatienceBearingWithOneAnotherInLove.

CHICKEN LYRICS — JAY SHARPE

This week, prepare your heart and mind to be everything that God has called you to be. Operate & excel within your realm!

Never cry over spilt milk, the end of a bad relationship, or a missed flight.

There comes a time when you have to let go of what you are getting and grab a hold of what you deserve! #Whoosah.

CHICKEN LYRICS   **JAY SHARPE**

When you focus on the good in others it will bring out the best in you. #BeBlessed~

Hatred is as weak as what it does, it changes nothing; but Love, love has the power to cover a multitude of things and it changes everything.

CHICKEN LYRICS   **JAY SHARPE**

''Let not your heart be troubled today.' We are not able to control or change the things around us, but we can guard and protect what's on the inside of us. Do not feel insecure about the things you cannot change. What's the point?
#LearnHowToCope~

You have the power to TURN IT AROUND! Make it a great day!

Healthy mind equates to a healthy life.

CHICKEN LYRICS   **JAY SHARPE**

The only way you can completely fail is if you never ever try.

Let go of the fear and start thinking about the endless possibilities! #Focus #Push #Try

Love what you are doing until you can start doing what you love.

There are no bad words, only bad expressions.

The language of the world is love. Once you learn to speak that language you will never utter or express a bad word.

Every successful woman knows her worth.

CHICKEN LYRICS JAY SHARPE

There are some things that he does that I don't like, but he is everything I love.

Leave the haters and the naysayers right there on your page. Let them watch you soar to new heights. The more hot air that comes out of their mouth, the more they will flame your great big balloon for success.

Sometimes you just have to let folks tell their truth and live their lie.

It's not easy coming into an environment everyday where people expect you to fail and setup obstacles to ensure that you do. Do yourself a favor get out and go where people expect you to thrive.

CHICKEN LYRICS **JAY SHARPE**

Your abundant life is wrapped up in your purpose. Find your purpose and start living abundantly!

If you think that you are lonely now, wait until you choose the wrong people to be around.

CHICKEN LYRICS   **JAY SHARPE**

Give yourself permission to fail forward. Mistakes are simply 'Miss Takes'. Try again.

I wish more people would get in the habit of doing what's right instead of doing the right thing.

I'm not trying to be the best trainer you have ever had. It's more important to me to be the best person that ever trained you.

Life didn't happen to you, you happened to life. The evolution of life remains the same Birth, Journey, Death. You are responsible for the journey.

The most fashionable attire you can wear is a great attitude.

CHICKEN LYRICS **JAY SHARPE**

God will never give you something that was meant for someone else.

The act of willingness is one of the most powerful quality you can display in your lifestyle.

Whatever you do, don't stop until you cross over the finish line.

CHICKEN LYRICS   **JAY SHARPE**

Repeat after me *"I am good at loving people."*

We become good at what we can do but we become Pro's at what we love to do.

All PRO's have a common trait-PROfessional, PROactive, PROducer, PROficient.

I don't think my mind is ever asleep. Even when I'm sleeping my mind is dreaming.

CHICKEN LYRICS — JAY SHARPE

What matters most is the heart. Love loves lovers.

What if? What if you allow yourself to let go and feel the magic?

The only religion I practice is LOVE.

No one will follow a leader who is not willing to be lead.

The impact may have bruised me but it also inspired me.

When you lift up others, you experience a natural high.

Today is the best day to have a great day!

If you do not teach your kids how to discover their purpose, they will forever struggle trying to fit in with someone else's.

Grow with the FLOW~ Friendship, Leadership, Ownership & Worship~

CHICKEN LYRICS **JAY SHARPE**

"I can't" is suicide of the mind.

Only when you say *"I can't"* are you defeated.

Regardless of the person, place or things that is making you sad right now, take a moment and stop and think of a reason to smile anyway. Give yourself permission to let go of the sadness and replace it with a happy smile. It's okay. Letting go does not mean forgetting the pain. It simply means you are growing and becoming stronger and you are giving yourself approval to heal.

CHICKEN LYRICS

It's when you are right at that moment of your breakthrough, the adversary creeps up and tries to steal your joy. Today, I encourage you to HOLD ON! Have faith, pray, stay on task and reap the benefits of your hard work. Be strong!

CHICKEN LYRICS **JAY SHARPE**

Unity is not the same as uniformity, where everyone has to be the same or unanimity where we all have to agree. Unity is focusing on the things that unite us rather than the things that divide us. Let's move forward and become mature and help each other. Look for opportunities to build up rather than tearing down. To serve than being served. To learn from each other instead of clamoring for the teaching stand. Then we can be unified.

CHICKEN LYRICS   **JAY SHARPE**

We all want healthy relationships (Marriage Friendship, Community, Church etc.) First we need to become whole and healthy ourselves, since a relationship can only be as healthy as the least healthy person in it. A candid and realistic approach...each of us must aim to become a more complete person by recognizing our blind spots, learn to be authentic, strengthen our social skills and put the past in perspective.

Today I choose to make every effort to affiliate myself with affirmation of kindness, humility and love. I will do all possible to secede from all negativity.

When you open up your heart to helping others, the Universe accepts that as an invitation to join you and increase the possibilities.

When you help others to develop themselves, you also develop along the way.

CHICKEN LYRICS　　　　　　　　　　　　　　　　**JAY SHARPE**

Never become jealous of others blessings. God has a gift design especially for you.

The attack impacted me, the pain influenced me. But the lesson inspired me.

CHICKEN LYRICS **JAY SHARPE**

The mind reacts. The physical reenact. The soul responds.

It's important that when we are tested, to pass the test. Otherwise chances are you will have to retake the test.

There is a miracle in HOPE. Trust the process.

CHICKEN LYRICS   **JAY SHARPE**

Don't let people's perceptions of you define who you are. Remember their impression is based on their beliefs not yours.

Quality will always produce quantity.

Confirm what you know and affirm who you are. 'Fearfully & Wonderfully made.'

CHICKEN LYRICS **JAY SHARPE**

If the opportunity isn't knocking, you need to get some hinges and put on a door. Preparation is the key! Unlock your potential.

Never look back, you'll never get anywhere. (inspired by Cidney Lyon)

Life is a game. God is the player. (Inspired by Cidney Lyon)

'With God all things are possible' and the same is true within you. Exercise the GOD in you!

Know your worth! To love and be loved is priceless!

Don't give others permission to abuse you by keeping silent. Speak up and stop them right in their tracks.

CHICKEN LYRICS **JAY SHARPE**

Don't just stand there. Stand up!

There's nothing more beautiful than a woman with a great attitude.

Those who speak out of anger only showcase their ignorance.

Speak with passion and showcase your intelligence.

Disrespect of any kind is never okay. It's an illness. Every time someone disrespects you, send them a *'Get well soon'* card.

Don't waste today with yesterday's worry. Concentrate on the moment and create memories for tomorrow.

Become a liberator! Give yourself the freedom to be you!

Achievers are Believers!

One of the best ways to reduce stress is to build up others. Encourage someone else.

You have to be present in your life. Take control of YOU! Learn to see yourself correctly.

Don't be a channel of idle chatter. Become the element of change.

I will because I want. I have because I give. I do because I care. I can because I am.

Preparation is the key to opening the door of **your** success.

Challenges come to make you stronger. Don't allow fear to cripple your ability to overcome the giant in front of you. Be strong and courageous. Gather all your strength, focus on the target, pull back and aim...

Stop trying to be perfect, it's a waste of time. Do what is purpose filled and you will be perfectly fine.

CHICKEN LYRICS   **JAY SHARPE**

Start your day with a praise and end it with gratitude. #Mindfulness & Kindness.

'Whoever angers you controls you.' Anger is misplaced fear. Learn to be bold and calm. Get your point across and stay in control. Do not let your anger outlast the day.

Procrastination is one of the biggest dream killers.

CHICKEN LYRICS   **JAY SHARPE**

When your burden gets heavy, don't focus on the burden, focus on how you are carrying it.

All it takes is one person to believe in you. Let that one person be YOU! Believe in yourself.

People will say what they want to say. Let them! You have to make sure you do what you have to do. Focus!

Egos hear what they want to hear, confidence listens and learns.

Judge me now because you're gonna have to grudge me later. Hater!

Don't be his experiment, when you can be someone's experience.

CHICKEN LYRICS — JAY SHARPE

If we want to live longer, we have to be willing to grow old.

How can you be righteous when you are so bent on being right?

I am a whole person alone, but I am totally wholesome with you by my side.

CHICKEN LYRICS   JAY SHARPE

Love is who I am; therefore, it's what I do. I was created to love!

Stars don't shine in the light.

I loathe people who wear their academic achievement as a weapon of mass destruction. #EducatedFools-GrowUp-PutYourBigGirlPantiesOn.

CHICKEN LYRICS   JAY SHARPE

If you have to constantly tell me about your academic catalogue, then you need a refund on your education. Show me what you have accomplished then I'll make a deposit in you.

Be encouraged. No matter what you are going through, know that *'This too shall pass.'* Life is a series of events. Each one has its own season. Do all possible to recognize when you are in season and harvest the best fruits from the crop. It's about growth and growing.

CHICKEN LYRICS   **JAY SHARPE**

---

40 hours per week of time. Invest it wisely and productively. 'Create. Motivate and inspire.'

Normal is **Out**-dated. Natural is **In**-spiring.

Never apologize or have guilty feelings about putting yourself first.

CHICKEN LYRICS   **JAY SHARPE**

Stop being so normal. Become a natural.

I dare you to love. Hate is easy for you because you are weak minded and it's easy for you to react than respond to your situation. You see, it takes courage to love. Love requires forgiveness and patience, gentleness. It's not boastful. It's not just words but actions. You say you are strong then I dare you to love.

Fear is not to be feared. It's the spirit of fear that is to be feared.

Every door of opportunity in life has a key. It's called preparation.

Why are you afraid of the dark? The Almighty have empowered you abundantly to shine through the darkness. You are a shining star!

Birth something new today.

Your passion is who you are. Discover your passion and discover self!

Everything birthed has a record. Keep a record of your goals, ideas and dreams then when it's time to give birth, you'll have a record of the journey.

CHICKEN LYRICS   **JAY SHARPE**

Ask for clarity in the face of confusion. Only when you are able to process the assignment will you be able to produce.

If you find yourself on a highway with naysayers and haters, switch lanes. In fact, don't just switch lanes, press on the gas. Lose them!

Leader is a position. Leadership is an action. Leading is doing. Being lead is an attitude.

You DNA is your Divine Natural Attributes. Stay connected to your highest self and allow your DNA to connect to your lineage.

I have no buttons for you to push today. I'm all zippered up.

Get excited about who you are. People are attracted to excitement.

CHICKEN LYRICS   **JAY SHARPE**

Your circle should never be so small that others aren't welcome in.

Exclusive is so prejudice!

Something tells me you're gonna become a class act some day!!

CHICKEN LYRICS **JAY SHARPE**

Do not focus on what has happened, or is happening to you, concentrate on who you have become or are becoming during or after the process.

Dare...just dare...!!!

CHICKEN LYRICS   **JAY SHARPE**

A message to my Hater:

Dear Hater,

*If you weren't my friend before Facebook, why would I accept your friend request now? Please go to my 'Fan Page' and 'like' to see how much I am loved by many or my 'Business Page' and watch my progress, OR you can just become a 'Follower' and see only what I **allow** you to see. 'GetYourLife!'*

Think about what is holding you back from achieving your highest you! Make a plan of action to rid yourself of the fear, distraction or the unwillingness to move forward. Creating a plan gives you a clear pathway towards your goal.

Never give up on a good thing! It may not be perfect, but if it's good for you, then that's all that matters. There's no perfect thing, but loving a good thing is perfect. ~

CHICKEN LYRICS   **JAY SHARPE**

'Become the change you want to see.' If the people, places and/or things around you are not what you want, make the change.

There comes a time when you have to be the change.

While they talk, you keep moving forward. With every word they utter, you keep on moving forward and before you know it, you will be so far out of earshot and they will only see your trail.

CHICKEN LYRICS   JAY SHARPE

My hands have been too crooked to be pointing fingers straight at anyone. *"He who is without sin cast the first stone."*

Sometimes you have to get in the ring and fight with all your might and rest, and then get up and fight again. Then even when you feel like giving up you throw one last punch and that may do the trick. *Galatian 6:9 *'and let us not grow weary of doing good, for in due season we will reap, if we do not give up.*

Freedom is such a costly attribute. John 3:16 *'"For God so loved the world, that he gave his only Son.*

In business, back to the basic makes cent$.

Hypocrisy is your blurred vision of others.
*Matthew 7:29 *"You hypocrite, first take the log out of your own eye, and then you will see clearly to take the speck out of your brother's eye.*

CHICKEN LYRICS **JAY SHARPE**

Coulda, woulda, shoulda….the voice of procrastination! *Proverbs 13:14 *'The soul of the sluggard craves and gets nothing, while the soul of the diligent is richly supplied.*

The sky is the limit, but some of us never look up! *Mark 9:23 *'And Jesus said to him, "If you can! All things are possible for one who believes."*

Fear is the most captive prison!

You are only as good as your mind says you are.
*Hebrew 10:35 *'Therefore do not throw away your confidence, which has a great reward.'*

Any girl can be a bride. It takes a woman to become a good wife. *Proverbs 31:10 *"An excellent wife who can find? She is far more precious than jewels.*

CHICKEN LYRICS JAY SHARPE

Sometimes we quietly suffer on the inside, while still showing a bright smile on the outside. Tap into your feelings. Deal with the emotion at face value and put it in check rather than cover it over with pretense. Let truth be told.

It takes willingness to create an action that will generate a mighty reaction.

CHICKEN LYRICS **JAY SHARPE**

Know what is important in life. I've never seen a tombstone that reads, "Here lays *'John Doe'*. He had three houses, five cars and millions in the bank." *Matthew 6:33 *'But seek first the kingdom of God and his righteousness, and all these things will be added to you.*

CHICKEN LYRICS   **JAY SHARPE**

Stop focusing so much on what others do or don't do. Concentrate on the task that you have been given. Work towards doing a 'mighty much' with what you have. * Jeremiah 29:11 *'For I know the plans I have for you, declares the LORD, plans to prosper you and not to harm you, plans to give you hope and a future.'*

CHICKEN LYRICS   **JAY SHARPE**

Fire with fire becomes a blaze. Learn how to stay calm in the midst of chaos. Rely on that infinite ability, divine wisdom and still voice. Prayer works in all situations. Prayer signals Heaven to appoint the right MAN for the job. * *Psalm 46:10 'Be still and know that I am God!'*

CHICKEN LYRICS   JAY SHARPE

I think all relationships are complicated.
I think all marriages have their ups & downs.
I think all families are dysfunctional.
I think all churches have saints and sinners.
I think every workplace have drama.
I think everyone's life is a challenge.
What I do know is that we are all humans and we all share these experiences...that's life! *Romans 12: 4-5 *'For as in one body we have many members, and the members do not all have the same function, so we, though many, are one body in Christ, and individually members one of another.*

CHICKEN LYRICS   **JAY SHARPE**

You don't have to engage in every battle that comes your way. Some folks want to fight with you just so they can get in the same ring. Know your league and stay focus in your arena.

It's gonna be okay. Don't react to whatever is out of sync around you right now; instead, breathe, think, refocus and then respond. The result will be much better.'

CHICKEN LYRICS   **JAY SHARPE**

For every failure there is a lesson. *Corinthians 10:13 *'God is faithful, and he will not let you be tempted beyond your ability, but with the temptation he will also provide the way of escape, that you may be able to endure it.'*

If I take my eyes off the prize, I have already lost. Game over!

CHICKEN LYRICS   JAY SHARPE

I have learned not to fight fire with fire, hate with hate, evil with evil, but that I have to fight with a force stronger than my opponent's, even it is only my will to live.

It's when you are at the very point of giving up; *'Wallah'* a breakthrough appears. Hang in there, it gets better. #Determination

Practice to never lose. Even in a physical defeat there can be a mental win. Learn from your mistakes.

Passion always trumps excuses. Stay on task.

Today the choice is yours! Make every effort to affiliate yourself with affirmations of kindness, humility and love. Then do all possible to secede from all negativity.

Say it with me. *"No matter how gloomy this day may seem, I am looking at it with bright eyes and a bushy tail! My attitude will determine how far I rise above the gloominess. I will rise!"*

Don't allow others to tell you who you are and what you should be. If you need help, go to the reference guide that gives you all the details. It's called the BIBLE- *'Basic Life Instructions Before Leaving Earth'*~

Learn to love life and all its possibilities! Stop holding LOVE hostage and demanding a ransom! Love is unconditional! Live! Love! Laugh! & Learn!

Today, center your thoughts on the excellence of The Almighty's creation. Take the time to see all the beauty that surrounds you.

CHICKEN LYRICS   **JAY SHARPE**

Stop paying attention to negativity; you are only giving it more energy. You are doing great! Refocus on the positive!

Live Simply. Love Completely. Care Deeply. Speak Kindly... Leave The Rest to God!"

If you stand up for something at least believe in it! *James 1:22 *"But be doers of the word, and not hearers only, deceiving yourselves."*

CHICKEN LYRICS **JAY SHARPE**

You cannot change anyone, you can only change you and hope that the change in you, will impact and influence others to make a change within them. *Matthew 5: 13-16 *'You are the light of the world. A city set on a hill cannot be hidden. Nor do people light a lamp and put it under a basket, but on a stand, and it gives light to all in the house. In the same way, let your light shine before others, so that they may see your good works and give glory to your Father who is in heaven.'*

CHICKEN LYRICS **JAY SHARPE**

Leave them haters and naysayers right there on your page. Let them watch you soar going forward. The more hot air that comes out of their mouth is the more they will flame your great big balloon for success! #AnticipatingTheRideUpUp&Away~
Matthew 10v22:' And you will be hated by all for my name's sake. But the one who endures to the end will be saved'

Garner a mentality like an eagle. Fly above your adversaries and soar towards your possibilities!
*Joshua 1:9 *'Have I not commanded you? Be strong and courageous. Do not be frightened, and do not be dismayed, for the Lord your God is with you wherever you go."*

CHICKEN LYRICS   **JAY SHARPE**

Your Mind, Body & Soul must operate in harmony. One cannot be off balance; hence your very being will be incapable of achieving the highest you.
*John 14v6: *'Jesus said to him, "I am the way, and the truth, and the life. No one comes to the Father except through me.*

Learn how to NOT become a retaliator to negativity, haters, and naysayers. It will confuse your enemies as well as the 'frenemies'; you will experience a high that only eagles can relate to. Fly above the meaningless~#SoarOn

CHICKEN LYRICS JAY SHARPE

You can make a difference! All you have to do is believe it, become it and do it!
#BeTheChangeYouWantToSee~

I believe in miracles, and luck and blessings and opportunities and favors and preferences and choices... all I have to do is be prepared.
#PostionedToProsperRainOnMe~

CHICKEN LYRICS   **JAY SHARPE**

"How can you want to be like all the others and call yourself real? Be you! Live Your Truth! Anything less than that is a lie!"

#EmbraceTheAuthenticYou~

You have the power to TURN IT AROUND! Make it a great day!

CHICKEN LYRICS **JAY SHARPE**

Don't you feed into that negative energy! Defuse it! THINK positive!

The road to success does not come without incidents and yes, sometimes even accidents. Be prepared for what lies ahead of you. Equip yourself with the tools & resources needed for the journey. Wherever life may take you, always ensure that your vision is 20/20.
#TeamFocusPrepared&Determine!

Jealousy is a nasty & terrible disease! #FindACure~

CHICKEN LYRICS   JAY SHARPE

Diligence is one of the best work attire~

Get mad enough not to quit! Remind yourself of how far you have come......and keep moving forward. #Determination~

Friendly Reminder! Pay attention to signs and patterns. Nothing epic happens without them.'

CHICKEN LYRICS   **JAY SHARPE**

Moving on and moving forward are two different choices. #KeepPushing

Exodus 14: 15-16 *'The Lord said to Moses, "Why do you cry to me? Tell the people of Israel to go forward. Lift up your staff, and stretch out your hand over the sea and divide it, that the people of Israel may go through the sea on dry ground.'*

Fall asleep with a dream and wake up with a vision. Habbakuk 2:2 "And the **Lord** answered me: "Write the vision; make it plain on tablets, so he may run who reads it."

Why must you settle when you can make another choice?

Happy Mind-Happy Life! #LOL~ :-))
'Romans 12:12 *'Do not be conformed to this world, but be transformed by the renewal of your mind, that by testing you may discern what is the will of God, what is good and acceptable and perfect.'*

Some of us need to break up with the negativity and start a relationship with the positive.

Some of us have broken up with the negative person but continue to have a relationship with the negativity they have left behind. Let go!

Become a witness for your soul. Tell yourself the truth, the whole truth and nothing but the truth so help you God! ~#TheTruthShallSetYouFree~

CHICKEN LYRICS   **JAY SHARPE**

If you are able to sit in the reality, then you must be brave enough to stand in the truth!

It's the end of yet another week. Give yourself a round of applause for making it thus far. Reflect on the past week and give credit where credit is due. Then prepare one-self to embrace all the possibilities of the week ahead.
#ForgetAboutTheNegative #FocusOnThePositive~

CHICKEN LYRICS   **JAY SHARPE**

I have a responsibility to continue creating work for my haters by being successful.

It is my job to keep my haters employed by continuing to be successful. After all, what will they do if I don't? #KeepThemTalking

Get over yourself! The path to success lies in coping. Learn how to sit still and deal with the real you. Absorb your thoughts and learn to process them into positive actions. This is mandatory if you want others to cope with you.

Once you get a clear vision of what you are created to do, it's becomes your responsibility to make that vision a reality. Passion-Persistence-Pursuit~

CHICKEN LYRICS   **JAY SHARPE**

Never underestimate the power of 'Willingness'

Stop hanging out with people who have poor mental hygiene, sooner or later their stench will rub off on you.

Life has no way of becoming better until you begin to do so.

Stop trying to hide the masterpiece God has made. Come out of your hiding place.

Find someone who can be happy without you but would prefer to share their happiness with you~

Go ahead! Reveal the real you~

Understand that being the 'greatest you' is a lifestyle. It's an ongoing process. ~

If only you knew how great you are, you would stop accepting the limitations others try to put on your life. Take Control! #BecomeTheGreatestYou~

CHICKEN LYRICS   **JAY SHARPE**

Happiness is a lifestyle.

Change can be a fearful thing...but how we handle the change determines how progressive we will become. #EmbraceTheChange #Evolve

Don't allow others hatred to stop your love. Everyone needs love, even the haters. #LoveIsTheAnswer~

When you free your mind of distractions, negativity and clutter the possibilities are endless! #HealthyMindHealthyLife

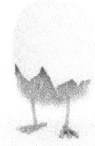

People are quick to say, *"I have lots of wisdom, or I am wise."* Then they start to judge or try to be right at all times. You are lacking understanding of what wisdom is. A wise person gets a broader and deeper understanding of a person, place, circumstance or thing. #BroadenYourHorizon~

'With wisdom get understanding. `Wisdom is not about soundness of judgment or right use of knowledge. It's more about having a deeper, broader understanding of life.

Wanting what others have or trying to be like others is normal, but definitely not natural. Everything natural births something authentic! If you want what others have or want to be like them, then you are simply duplicating the other person and stifling the authentic you. Step into your Natural!

Just a little love can change a multitude of things! #ShowSomeLoveToday.

Having the ability to do something and the will to do something are two very different things! #WillingnessMattersWillingnessCounts~.

CHICKEN LYRICS — JAY SHARPE

Every time a woman speaks negatively of another woman she reverts our progress of feminism.

The more we learn about ourselves is the more we recognize our preferences and our prejudices will slowly subside. There are a lot of others in us and us in others.

'Stop praying for surviving through anything in your life. Pray a stronger and more specific prayer. Pray that you LIVE 'in' all circumstances. You are alive so LIVE!'

Allowing others to tell you who you are, is denying your divine lineage.

An attempt is your first step towards progress.

Live a life of possibilities rather than probabilities.
Chances are you will make better choices.

CHICKEN LYRICS **JAY SHARPE**

Teach your kids about love, how to love themselves and others! Show them love and how to love, so that they can recognize it, feel it, express it and believe it, as receivers and givers! The worst thing that can happen to someone is becoming a grownup and never knowing what love is. #AllWeNeedIsLove ♥

CHICKEN LYRICS   **JAY SHARPE**

It doesn't matter who you are and how well you do 'it'. You will never be able to please everyone! The longer you hold on to this illusion is the further away you are from achieving your 'it'. Like Nike says 'Just Do It!'

If you always expect the worst of everything, then be not surprise when your expectations are met! #ChickenLyrics~

CHICKEN LYRICS   **JAY SHARPE**

Spending quality time with your child/ren is essential to their upbringing. Every child should know that they are special, loved, respected and unique. Love on your children! If you are not a parent, there are thousands of children in this world who needs love. Volunteer some of your time to spend with a child.

"It's a New Day! Grab a hold of its possibilities!"

CHICKEN LYRICS **JAY SHARPE**

In the game of life, people are going to talk regardless if you win or lose. Keep them talking by mastering the game. Go for the trophy! The last time I checked only WINNERS get the trophies! #GoForIt~.

Only you can stop yourself from reaching your full potential! No one can take that away from you unless you give them permission to. #PreserveYourRight~.

When they say" No you can't"; You say "Yes I can". Don't be stubborn and rebellious. Show them you are persistent and determine. #TeamOvercomer!

Surround yourself with people who have good intentions towards you. Not everyone who appears to be good to you is good for you. Pay attention to their intention. Make sure they are for you and not just with you.
#BeAwareOfThePowerOfIntention~

You have the power and the ability to create the space, experiences and lifestyle you want. There is a force that is specifically in alignment with you to make it happen. You are empowered by The Almighty! #Confidence~

Know that there is always a way. You just have to be willing enough to find it!
#TheJourneyContinues~

CHICKEN LYRICS   **JAY SHARPE**

By the way, it's gonna be okay. Stop worrying about it so much. #CoachThySelf!

'Let the haters hate, that's their job. Yours is to focus and keep moving forward.' #KeepYourEyesOnThePrize~

Build Baby Build!! Develop your self-worth so you can increase your net-worth! #CharacterCounts~

There are people who can't be happy for you when you move ahead. These are the type of people you want to limit your interaction with. I never completely rule out people out of my life because I believe they are there as a lesson or a blessing... however, when I learn my lesson I keep it moving and try to teach others about the lessons learned. On the other hand, folks who come as a blessing I do all possible to keep them close to my heart and become a blessing to them and others as well.

CHICKEN LYRICS   **JAY SHARPE**

Confidence should be worn like a well-tailored suit. Poised and cut to fit!

There are people who are not able to handle your success. They are lacking self-worth and discipline. Be intolerant of them and the negative energy they bring around you. Corinthians 5:11 *'But actually, I wrote to you not to associate with any so-called brother if he is an immoral person, or **covetous**.*

Be in a relationship where quitting is not an option.
Philippians 4:13 *'I can do all things through him who strengthens me.*

Practice saying 'I Love You' more often. Start by looking in the mirror.

If you wake up, everything is possible!
Thessalonians 5:21 'But test everything; hold fast what is good.'

CHICKEN LYRICS   **JAY SHARPE**

I never worry about being loved. My very existence assures me each day that I am loved. I concern myself more with giving and showing love to others, that's what matters most.

Older women, support younger women
Remember you were once them!

If only we mirror the mind of an eagle………wow! How far we can soar!

CHICKEN LYRICS   JAY SHARPE

Replace your evil eyes with an eagle eye.

Eagles hardly ever fly in flocks; they soar high above on their own.

CHICKEN LYRICS

JAY SHARPE

Eagles are used to being pushed! They are taught since birth. That's how they conquer their fear and fly high up above.

Make a plan, stick to it and execute! Job well done!

Gone are the days where I am crippled by the inability of someone to love me.

CHICKEN LYRICS   **JAY SHARPE**

Make all your dreams come true. Never stop dreaming.

Today, know that whatever is happening to you right now is happening at the right moment.

I'm not secretive; you just haven't earned the right to my privacy settings.

CHICKEN LYRICS   **JAY SHARPE**

You don't have to keep secrets, just simply adjust your privacy settings to your liking.

Clear out the clutter! Mind, Body & Spirit need structure.

People who hurt you for no reason, is revealing their true self. Believe them.

There are basically two emotions in this world. Love & Fear. Everything that is loved cannot be feared and everything that is feared cannot be loved.

Everything that is good for you is outside of your comfort zone. #Step out

CHICKEN LYRICS   **JAY SHARPE**

The decision you made was the right one. Where you are right now is where you need to be. 'Be still and know that The Almighty is working in your favor.'

It's an amazing experience when we remove prejudice from our eyes and start looking at others through the windows of our heart and soul. We are all created equal. The difference we see in each other are from the choices we make.

There is no change without commitment.

CHICKEN LYRICS — JAY SHARPE

Don't allow your past tense to show up in your present tense, this will only cause a pretense.

Willingness is the first step towards change.

Insinuating is for cowards. Bravery is saying what you mean.

CHICKEN LYRICS JAY SHARPE

The positive changes you make in your life are tied to your purpose.

Lie about you and you will lie about me.

You don't have to change who you are to change where you are.

Your purpose is wrapped up in your fear.

If you are giving the same type of help to the same type of people repeatedly, you are an enabler. You are not helping them to grow.

'As is' is very different than *'As I am.'*

Body

CHICKEN LYRICS JAY SHARPE

Body:

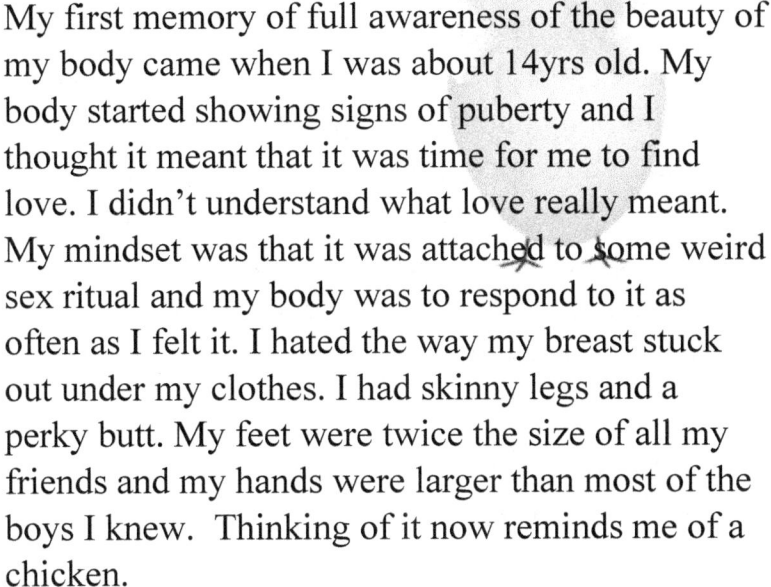

My first memory of full awareness of the beauty of my body came when I was about 14yrs old. My body started showing signs of puberty and I thought it meant that it was time for me to find love. I didn't understand what love really meant. My mindset was that it was attached to some weird sex ritual and my body was to respond to it as often as I felt it. I hated the way my breast stuck out under my clothes. I had skinny legs and a perky butt. My feet were twice the size of all my friends and my hands were larger than most of the boys I knew. Thinking of it now reminds me of a chicken.

As I grew older, I started getting lots of attention via compliments, stares, questions, critiques from boys and girls alike for the exact body features that I detested. I started wondering *"hmmmm...maybe there is something interesting"* and I needed to find it. I would lock myself in the very bedroom where I wrote most of my thoughts and slowly begin to explore my body. I would take a broken piece of mirror (having a full length mirror was a luxury back then.) angled it to where I could view my entire body and begin my research. It felt good and I started to appreciate every single feature of my body…I discovered that my body was truly invaluable and I made a vow to do all possible to love it more than anyone else ever could…with the exception of my feet…that came at a much later date.

Accepting our body, the way God created it, is vital to your existence. The body was given as a vessel to carry the thoughts and emotions of the mind and spirit. It represents! It is a reflection of a deeper us. It expresses every thought, every emotion, and every experience we have. Treat it well!

CHICKEN LYRICS　　　　　　　　　　　　　　**JAY SHARPE**

I am perfectly imperfect and my imperfection is perfectly perfect.

'To everything there is a season'. Never stay longer than your season with people, place or thing.

CHICKEN LYRICS　　　　　　　　　　　　　　　　　　　**JAY SHARPE**

Staying indoors today can be just as productive as any other day. Take a moment to write down your goals. Reflect on your past thoughts, actions and results. Take note of the triumphs and the lessons learned. Use both lists as a benchmark moving forward. Set your goal to your highest self. Envision yourself operating in that realm. Make it realistic and create an action plan to achieve it.

Stop being so cheap with the truth that your honesty has to pay the price!

Not everything that makes you feel good is good for you.

Knowing is faith, belief is action. Believe in what you know in order to take action. *'Faith without works is dead.'*

Never lose who you are for what people think you are.

If you want to **hear** me speak, then you have to **listen** to what I have to say.

CHICKEN LYRICS   **JAY SHARPE**

Funny how everyone wants to live longer but no one wants to grow old.

Drama is so outdated! Get current!

Take a selfie! Be you!

When faced with a big task, break it into small parts and attack it piece by piece. Soon it will all come together. *'Rome wasn't built in a day.'*

CHICKEN LYRICS   **JAY SHARPE**

Being comfortable with your body is a fashion statement all on its own.

I hope I get the privilege of growing old.

You have to produce. Show thy fruits. *Matthew 7:16 *"You will recognize them by their fruits.*

CHICKEN LYRICS **JAY SHARPE**

Try talking to people instead of talking about them.
#A gossip betrays a confidence...
*Proverbs 11:12-13.

Without laughter everything would seems so dull.
Laughter is happiness articulated.

Learn how to dance in the rain~#FeelTheMagic~

CHICKEN LYRICS   **JAY SHARPE**

There is instant satisfaction in loving yourself!

You must do the work! Plain and simple! It's not gonna happen any other way! Do the work, get the reward! #WorkSmartPlayHard~

CHICKEN LYRICS   **JAY SHARPE**

Never allow others to constantly take you for granted. Become unavailable to them. #NoRegretsNoApology~

Take (5) five minutes out of your day and create a moment between you and your creator. Say a prayer of thanksgiving of five things you are grateful for thus far. #CountYourBlessings~

CHICKEN LYRICS **JAY SHARPE**

If you give up now, all your efforts would have been in vain. Acts 20:24 'But I do not account my life of any value nor as precious to myself, if only I may finish my course and the ministry that I received from the Lord Jesus, to testify to the gospel of the grace of God.'

I can't think of a better way to say 'I Love You' than with a home cook meal.

When it comes to my body, 'All rights reserved'.

Remember if people talk behind your back it simply means you are two steps ahead!

CHICKEN LYRICS JAY SHARPE

In a relationship, when needs are not met, people will do what they want.

Be careful where you store your crap because when the cesspool is full, it will run over and embarrass you. The heart is meant for love not hate.

Love your body and every feature of it!

CHICKEN LYRICS   **JAY SHARPE**

Be good to yourself. Spend some time taking care of your temple. It's the only vehicle you will have for the journey called life.

Do not harbor strife, anger, jealousy or ill emotions it will only destroy your body.

Every fashion is not for you. Just as not every furniture will suit your home. Accentuate your body with the style that best for you~

All houses are not built the same and all bodies are not created the same.

Get your daily dose of laughter; it's like pure vitamin for your body.

Style is who you are, fashion is what you want to be like.

Create a style that's unforgettable.

Young ladies, when it to comes to your bodies it's a valuable gift. Make sure the person that opens your gift appreciates it.

CHICKEN LYRICS   **JAY SHARPE**

There is a beautiful wind blowing your way whoooooooooeeoeeiii... feel the presence of The Almighty.
#SomethingGoodIsGoingToHappenToYou

As my children grew older, the more I enjoyed being a mother and the better I became at it.

It is important to let your children know that you love them. No one else can teach them that better than you.

CHICKEN LYRICS   JAY SHARPE

The best way to please God is to be yourself.

Learn to be bold. LOL- Live Out Loud
Laugh Out Loud!
Learn Out Loud!
Love Out Loud!

CHICKEN LYRICS   **JAY SHARPE**

Treat people with respect, even if they don't deserve it... but you do! #RespectYourself.

Each day on an hourly basis, you have 24 opportunities to do something positive.

CHICKEN LYRICS **JAY SHARPE**

You can send a thousand positive messages in a simple smile.

You have to do your part...It's that simple.
#StayFocused
#NeverGiveUp#DoTheWork#SweetReward.~

CHICKEN LYRICS　　　　　　　　　　　　　　　　　　　　**JAY SHARPE**

Before you see the change, you must become the change.

"It's really okay to be who you are...really, it is!"

Loving is the easy part...liking, is where the real work begins.

CHICKEN LYRICS — JAY SHARPE

What actions are you taking today to make your future look brighter? If you could catch a glimpse of your future would you like what you see?

Some of the largest prisons are built because of fame.

CHICKEN LYRICS   **JAY SHARPE**

"Please, Thank you, & I Appreciate You" are simply some of the most powerful words that will get you through some difficult times.

You are the only one who has the ability to change what you see in the mirror.

Whatever you do, always remember to take good care of you.

I don't know why we try so hard to be normal, when natural is so much more exciting!
#BeingYOU~

Be mature enough to love beyond the physical. Internal beauty never fades; it gets finer with age.

CHICKEN LYRICS   **JAY SHARPE**

We really don't have to figure it all out at once. Learn how to prioritize. Handle the urgent issues and organize the important stuff! It will all work out in the end.

So what if it didn't work out on the 1st, 2nd and 3rd try? Try again. You only fail when you don't try!

CHICKEN LYRICS   **JAY SHARPE**

Today's Thought:
If you are living your DREAM----Kudos to you!

Open your heart & close your mouth!'
#ChantDungPrejudice.

*John 13: 34-35 *"A new commandment I give to you, that you love one another: just as I have loved you, you also are to love one another. By this all people will know that you are my disciples, if you have love for one another."*

CHICKEN LYRICS   **JAY SHARPE**

Don't be the *chick* that he moved on to....be the *chick* he moved forward for.
#BecomeTheChoiceNotTheOption
*Isaiah 62 3:4 *'You shall be a crown of beauty in the hand of the **Lord**, and a royal diadem in the hand of your God. You shall no more be termed Forsaken, and your land shall no more be termed Desolate, but you shall be called My Delight Is in Her, and your land Married; for the **Lord** delights in you, and your land shall be married. '.

Remember you have the power! Today look the adversary straight in the eye and say *"Not today and tomorrow ain't looking any better."*

Preparation, Practice and Purpose are three great attributes to have.

CHICKEN LYRICS   **JAY SHARPE**

If you are speaking to others about another person more than you are speaking to the person, then the other person is not the problem, you are.

I love being a woman, and I especially love being a black woman. #LovingTheSkinI'mIn.

Get tested and see the results!

Love does not hurt. It's the abuse of love that hurts.

Spirit

Spirit:

'The nonphysical part of a person that is the seat of emotions and character.'

It was about 2:00 am and I was watching Dr. Myles Munroe on TV. As I listened to him speak about Kingdom Principles I was moved to tap into my deeper self and think about what does it mean to be spiritual with a Kingdom soul. That moment I heard the voice of God as I know it to be......'You are a spiritual being, you were created to be. You are a representation of me. I am the spirit within you, find your spirit and you will find me.'

'Seek ye first the Kingdom of God...'

It was at that very moment I decided that I need to know more about me. I need to understand the **AM** that **I AM**. I need to seek the Kingdom of God and represent it in the best way possible.

Over the years I have learned to feel the nonphysical part of me. To listen to the voices of the Universe as they come in the forms of a gentle breeze caressing my face, or a gush of wind that sweeps leaves in the air. I learn to listen to that still small voice in my ear...whispering...and connecting me to all and everything that I **AM**~

I vowed to continue to do all possible to practice only that which is good to my spirit. I find that thing to be love. Love is a many things…when the spirit of love attaches itself to something, the possibilities are endless. Love is a wonderful spirit!

My religion is LOVE. That's what I practice every day. Love makes me pray. Love makes me grateful. Love makes me worship. Love makes me love.

Religion is too close minded; I prefer to open my mind to being Spiritual and experience all God's people.

CHICKEN LYRICS   **JAY SHARPE**

When you are one with the Spirit there are no opposites.

How do you define prayer? Each time I open my mouth to speak I am praying. Praying with you, for you or having a conversation with God. Therefore, I need to be conscious and in the moment of love at all times.

God is able to do just THAT.

CHICKEN LYRICS   **JAY SHARPE**

Finding balance within can help you regulate your life. * "Peace I leave with you. My peace I give you. (John 14:27)

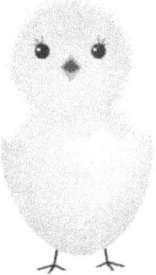

Every gift comes with a purpose. That purpose is attached to your talent and talent requires a skill. Find your purpose, use your talent and develop your skill. You are gifted!

CHICKEN LYRICS   **JAY SHARPE**

We must be careful not to interrupt God's plan for our lives. Exercise faith and trust the process.

God has given us sufficient time to find and live our purpose. Life can be long-term when we leave a legacy. There's life after death.

CHICKEN LYRICS   **JAY SHARPE**

Every fruit have a purpose. You are God's fruit, you have purpose.

Be a blessing to others and experience The Almighty blessings in your life.

Confidence is a weapon that destroys the lack thereof...

Every praise will carry you through a situation. *"Praise HIM while you can."*

CHICKEN LYRICS   **JAY SHARPE**

I believe that when we start looking at each other through the eyes of our hearts and souls, only then there will be peace.

The eyes in our heads see only what we are looking at. The heart sees what it feels and the soul sees what it knows.

I am all things possible!

CHICKEN LYRICS **JAY SHARPE**

Resist imitation and limitations! Go for the highest YOU!

There is nothing more authentic than your purpose.

Pay attention to the voice within. It's your most trusted friend.

Expect a blessing each day of your life.

CHICKEN LYRICS   **JAY SHARPE**

When you are blessed, you won't have to rely on miracles.

When you serve others according to the will of God and be a resource of comfort and peace for them, God will use you in ways you will never imagine and bless you with an overflow that is beyond compare. #VesselFullOfPower

Command your Mind, Body and Soul to work in harmony.

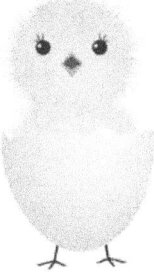

It's okay to be angry. It's never okay to hate.
*Ephesians 4:6 *'Be angry and do not sin; do not let the sun go down on your anger.'*

CHICKEN LYRICS — JAY SHARPE

You were born male and female. Being a man or a woman is a choice you have to make. * Galatians 6:5 *'for each will have to bear his own load.'*

If only you would Stop, Look & Listen to that who is within, you would be still, see and hear that which your purpose is. *Jeremiah 1:5 *'Before I formed you in the womb I knew you, and before you were born I consecrated you; I appointed you a prophet to the nations."*

Never let anyone 'Make your day'. God has already done that. Rejoice and be glad and ask others to join you along the way. * *Psalm 118:24 'This is the day that the lord has made, rejoice and be glad in it.'*

CHICKEN LYRICS   **JAY SHARPE**

Don't test God, trust God! *Proverbs 3:5 *Trust in the Lord with all your heart, and do not lean on your own understanding.*

Don't confuse my meekness for my weakness. My spirit is not flawed it is simply humble.

All it takes is a spark, to catch a fire and ignite a blaze! *Matthew 5: 13-16 *"You are the light of the world. A city set on a hill cannot be hidden.*

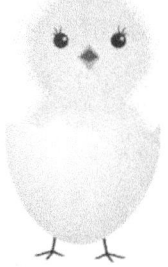

CHICKEN LYRICS   **JAY SHARPE**

Experience love in a responsible and selfless way. *Philippians 2:4 *'Let each of you look not only to his own interests, but also to the interests of others.*

You cannot be at your best with a corrupted mind, fill with thoughts of hate, & ugliness. The thoughts you harbor, has a direct impact on 'all of you' MIND, BODY & SPIRIT! Rid your mind of negativity, strife, fear, shame, ugliness, & hatred. Give yourself the gift of living. God gave your life, use it to be positive, happy, compassionate, courageous, loving, kind...*'Let go & let God'*~

*Ephesians 4:31-32.

CHICKEN LYRICS   **JAY SHARPE**

Sometimes you have to sacrifice yourself to allow others to thrive. #Selfless.

'I refuse to learn how to hate! Love is who I am; it is the essence of my being and the fuel for my existence.' #IAmStrongLikeThat!LetLoveLive!

CHICKEN LYRICS

JAY SHARPE

The presence of a storm is an indicator that God is present! <u>#Trust</u> #Hope #Praise #Worship~.

Today take a moment and give God praise! Acknowledge his presence all around you and come in agreement with HIM to be the best you~ #ShineOn~

CHICKEN LYRICS   **JAY SHARPE**

It is by FAITH that we make a difference.

Sometimes we love the right people for the wrong reasons & love the wrong people for the right reasons.'

'God favors those who *fayvah* (Reflects) HIM!'

"I have a dream that one-day LOVE will be the only power that rules the world."

PEACE...is the best therapy for your soul~.

I have a deep appreciation, admiration and love for sensible people, with good sense & sensibility! .#LiveEveryMoment!! #IAmALiver!! :-)

Leave a legacy that can heal, help or give hope to someone. Psalms 78:4 *'We will not hide them from their children, but tell to the coming generation the glorious deeds of the Lord, and his might, and the wonders that he has done.'*

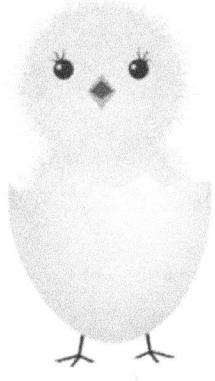

Live a lifestyle of kindness.

CHICKEN LYRICS   **JAY SHARPE**

All I know is that I believe in love, again and again and again…

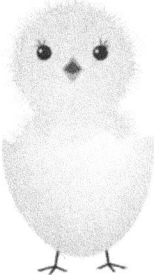

One of the best things a child can say to a parent is 'Thank You'.

Your karma is stronger than anyone's witchcraft. Be careful what you put out in the atmosphere.
Job 4:8 'As I have observed those who plow evil and those who sow trouble will reap it.'

CHICKEN LYRICS | **JAY SHARPE**

Stop trying to be the source. Your job is to co-create as the resource. Allow yourself to be the vessel of co-creation. You are already connected to the source. *1 Corinthians 8:6 'Yet for us there is but one God, the Father, from whom all things came and for whom we live; and there is but one Lord, Jesus Christ, through whom all things came and through whom we live.'*

CHICKEN LYRICS **JAY SHARPE**

There is a special place on earth created just for you. There is a special task design only for you. Your life matters! You were created for greatest! You are ordaining for excellence! You were made to be! No one and nothing can forfeit that! What are you waiting for...BECOME!

Rainbows are confirmations that you can go on.

It is by FAITH that we make a difference.

Make your supplication known to God. Sit back have faith and watch His mighty works.

CHICKEN LYRICS   **JAY SHARPE**

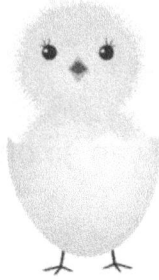

When we are operating in our purpose, doing what we do in purpose and on purpose we create impact and influence on the Universe. Affecting the effect of lives, takes purpose. You have to be willing to be in your purpose. Each time someone finds their purpose, a change occurs in the Universe. One person, one purpose infects us all. Your purpose is not yours; you are simply the vessel used to channel the change that will occur. You are equipped for the job; you were assigned by the Almighty! Finding your purpose change lives and revolutionizes the Universe.

God is within you, so in order to find God, you must look within.

Love cannot hurt, because God is love and God does not hurt.

The most beautiful piece of garment you can adorn is the Holy Spirit.

CHICKEN LYRICS   **JAY SHARPE**

Today's Prayer:
"Lord I am here to BE. Teach me your way and lead me closer to the "Am that I Am!"

CHICKEN LYRICS

JAY SHARPE